LOVE
yourself

This workbook belongs to

_____

Self-Love

Self-love is having regard for one's own well-being and happiness.

What is your own definition of self-love?

Understanding Self-Love

Accepting oneself completely, treating yourself with kindness and respect, and nurturing your growth and welfare are all examples of self-love.

Self-love involves your ideas and feelings about yourself, as well as how you treat yourself.

So, when you think of self-love, try to imagine what you'd do for yourself, how you'd talk to yourself, and how you'd feel about yourself if you truly loved and cared about yourself.

When you love yourself, you have a good outlook on life. This does not imply that you always feel good about yourself. That would be absurd! You can, for example, be sad, furious, or disappointed with yourself while still loving yourself.

What does Self-Love Look like?

Forgiving yourself when you mess up

MAKE *yourself* **A PRIORITY**

Not letting others take advantage of you

Asking for help without feeling off

YOUR *feelings* ARE VALID

Not holding unnecessary grudges

Saying positive things to yourself

Somethings that I love about myself

What does Self-Love Look like?

Making healthy choices for your body and mind

Holding yourself accountable

Recognizing your strengths and weaknesses

BE strong brave fearless

Challenging yourself

Noticing your progress and effort over perfection

LOVING ME

TODAY I LOVE MYSELF
BECAUSE

TODAY I FORGIVE MYSELF
BECAUSE

WAYS I SHOW MYSELF LOVE

I FEEL_____
BECAUSE

MY HOPE FOR TODAY IS

SELF LOVE GOALS

BODY GOALS

○ _____
○ _____
○ _____
○ _____
○

MIND GOALS

○ _____
○ _____
○ _____
○ _____
○

OTHER GOALS

○ _____
○ _____
○ _____
○ _____
○ _____
○

What is your happy place?

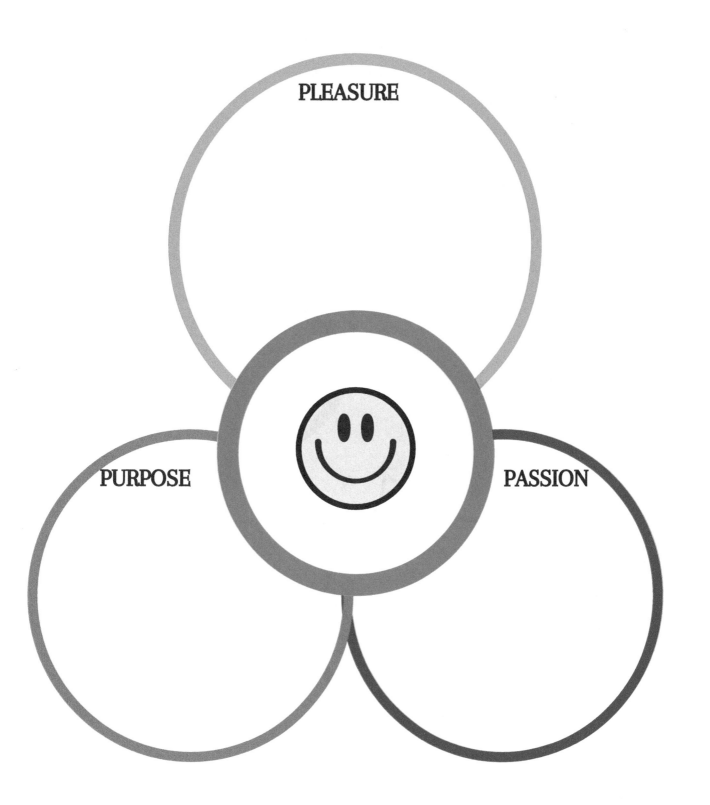

Affirmation Bubble

Use each bubble, to write out your favorite and go-to affirmations, and use these bubbles to repeat the affirmations to yourself each day.
The key to using affirmations is to say it with emotion and believe in every word you say.

⊕ Positive feelings I experienced today?

You CAN DO THIS

⊖ I had a negative thought about myself when

A positive though i can have next time is

Self-love: Focus on your Health

Motivation

- ♥ _____
- ♥ _____
- ♥ _____
- ♥ _____
- ♥ _____
- ♥ _____
- ♥ _____
- ♥ _____

Important

- ♥ _____
- ♥ _____
- ♥ _____
- ♥ _____
- ♥ _____
- ♥ _____
- ♥ _____
- ♥ _____

Where to start

Habits to Start

Habits to Stop

GROUNDING EXERCISE

1. Go to a quiet area in your home.

2. Rate your anxiety between 1 - 10.

3. Find a comfortable chair and sit up tall, with your spine straight and relaxing your shoulders.

4. Place your feet on the floor (barefoot).

5. Take slow deep breaths in and out until you form a rythm.

6. How many windows do you see?

7. How many doors do you see?

8. How many electrical devices do you see? Are any of them making noise? If so, what do they sound like?

9. What color is your top? What does the material feel like?

10. How does the chair you're sitting on feel like?

11. What does the floor feel like? Is it smooth or rough? Cold or warm? Hard or soft? Are there any imperfections on it? If so, what do you see?

12. What can you hear in the backgroun?

13. As you're breathing deeply, can you smell anything? Is it nice?

14. What kind of feeling do you have in your mouth right now? Can you taste anything?

15. Name your favorite TV show.

16. Name all the shapes you can think of.

17. Name the funniest movie you've ever watched.

18. Name your favorite countries.

19. Rate your anxiety between 1 - 10 again.

20. If it is still over a 5, repeat the exercise.

Affirmation Bubble

MIRROR MIRROR

What do you see when you look in the mirror?

I see someone who is

Forms of Self-Love

These are various forms of self-love, and these ways helps you be more in tune with your mind and body, show you how you can accept yourself and love yourself more, as well as giving you the boost of positivity and clarity to live an amazing life

 Nourish your body properly

Move your body
Keep active

 Stop Comparing Yourself to others

Forms of Self-Love

Be around
supportive people

Let go of Toxic
relationships

Step out of your
comfort Zone

Meditate and be in
tune with your mind

Self-love: Focus on your Health

Motivated

- ♥ _____
- ♥ _____
- ♥ _____
- ♥ _____
- ♥ _____
- ♥ _____
- ♥ _____
- ♥ _____

Important

- ♥ _____
- ♥ _____
- ♥ _____
- ♥ _____
- ♥ _____
- ♥ _____
- ♥ _____
- ♥ _____

Where to start

Habits to Start

Habits to Stop

Forms of Self-Love

What other forms of self-love do you know and wish to practice?

BE strong brave fearless

That Negative Side

Sometimes when you decide to get rid of all the rubbish and focus on your self-care and want to love yourself more, some form of negativity creeps inside your head.

It may be negative thoughts about who you were before and how you cannot do what you set out to do, or it may be negative words from the people closest to you. When this happens,

Don't Fret.

It is normal to have these all around you, but it is your

reaction to these thoughts and words that count.
Will you go back to the same old, boring, and no fun person you were, or will you push aside this negativity, look failure in the eyes and say you are ready?

IT IS UP TO YOU!!

Understand where this negativity is coming from.

Access yourself and write out where this negativity is coming from. It is important for you to know this, so you can know how to tackle it.

Wheel of Negativity

Write out the common negative thoughts that you tell yourself. Let it all out from the most talked about in your head to the least.

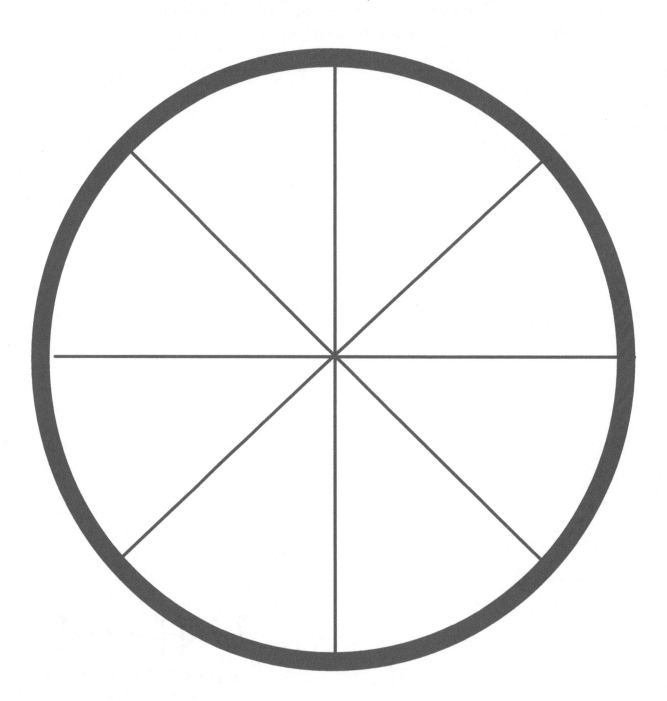

Wheel of Positivity

At this point, write out the positive words you say to yourself to conquer any from of negativity inside of you.

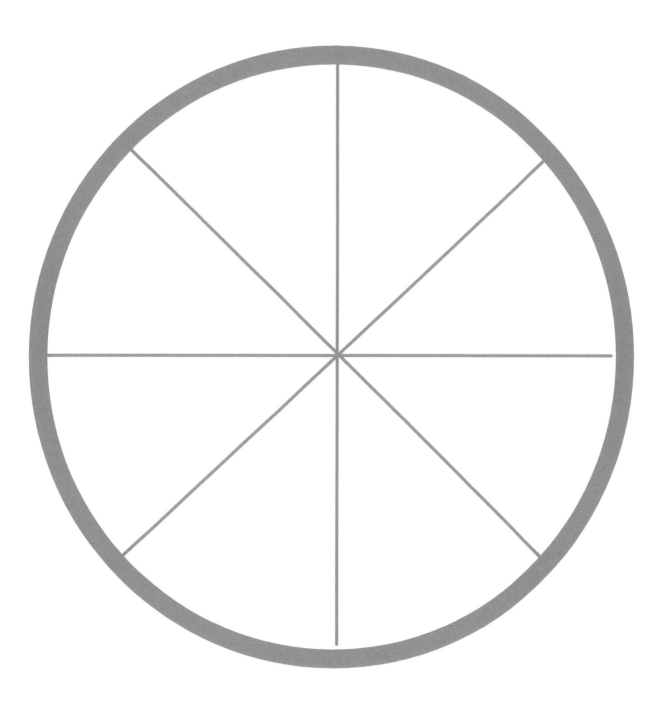

Wheel of more Positivity

If the positive words didn't fill that previous wheel, use this wheel to write out more and more positive words to yourself

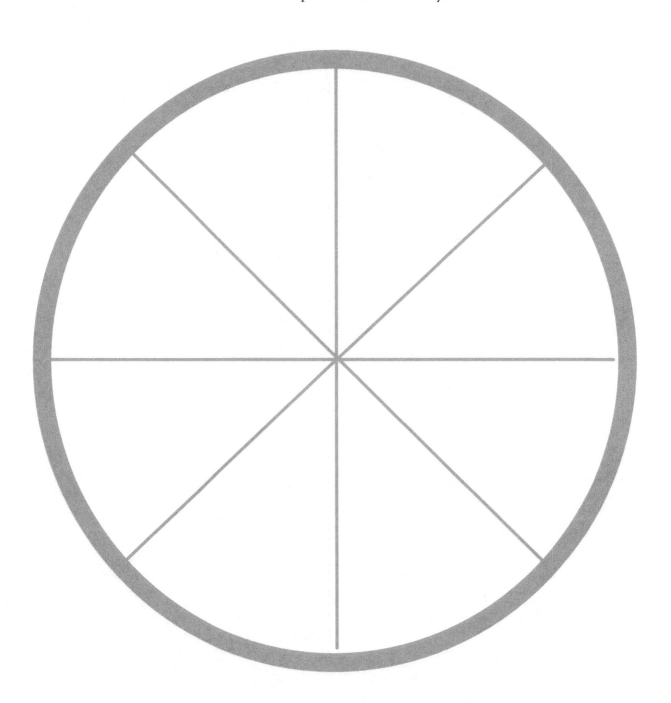

30 Days of Self Love Challenge

For the next 30 days, perform one act of self-love upon yourself and see how you feel about it

DAY 1 Buy yourself Flowers	Day 2 Write 5 short term goals for the month	DAY 3 Write down 5 things you love about yourself	Day 4 Go for a Jog, walk or a run	Day 5 Buy 1 thing you really want
Day 6 Try guided meditation	Day 7 Spend 1 hour in Nature	Day 8 Create a vision board for yourself	Day 9 Read a chapter of a book	Day 10 Get some extra sleep tonight
Day 11 Take a warm bath	Day 12 Host a game night with friends	Day 13 Do a random act of kindness for someone	Day 14 Do a stretch session	Day 15 Go to the sauna
Day 16 Unplug from your phone	Day 17 Declutter your space	Day 18 Make a nourishing meal	Day 19 Say No	Day 20 Write down 3 hard things you did today
Day 21 Change your environment in one way	Day 22 Wear an outfit that makes you feel good	Day 23 Watch an empowering movie	Day 24 Write a few things you are grateful for	Day 25 Do a digital cleanse
Day 26 Call up a good friend and chat	Day 27 Do something fun and exciting	Day 28 Develop an evening self-care routine	Day 29 Write down your future goals	Day 30 Treat yourself

Get to know you

How well do you know yourself? Answer these questions.

1.What is something you enjoy doing?

2. What is your biggest strength?

3. What is your biggest weakness?

4. What do you consider as your greatest achievement?

Get to know you

How well do you know yourself? Answer these questions.

5. What do you love about yourself?

6. What makes you happy?

7. What are your Triggers?

8. When do you feel the most confident?

Get to know you

How well do you know yourself? Answer these questions.

9. What do you need to let go of?

10. What positive changes do you need to make in your life?

11. What inspires you in your life?

12. How can you make your life more meaningful?

What do you love about yourself?

Self-Love Practices

This shows 4 areas of your life where you need to practice self-love. Fill these four areas with the self-love activity that you are practicing, or want to practice.

Emotional

Social

Physical

Spiritual

Self-Talk Log

Have an honest conversation with yourself.

Different
doesn't mean
wrong

Describe the person that you want to become only using verbs

Daily Reflection

What are 10 things you love about yourself?

_____

_____

_____

_____

_____

_____

_____

_____

_____

_____

_____

_____

_____

_____

_____

_____

_____

_____

_____

Daily Reflection

What do you believe self-love to be?

_____

_____

_____

_____

_____

_____

_____

_____

_____

_____

_____

_____

_____

_____

_____

_____

_____

_____

Daily Reflection

What is something unique about you?

_____

_____

_____

_____

_____

_____

_____

_____

_____

_____

_____

_____

_____

_____

_____

_____

_____

_____

Daily Reflection

In what little ways have you grown?

_____

_____

_____

_____

_____

_____

_____

_____

_____

_____

_____

_____

_____

_____

_____

_____

_____

_____

Daily Reflection

How do you make other people feel?

The Gift of Gratitude

It is important to be grateful for the little things in life because, with gratitude, you focus on the positive things in life rather than focusing on the negative things.

What am you grateful for?

What are your reasons for being grateful?

Daily Reflection

What habit do you need to give up?

_____

_____

_____

_____

_____

_____

_____

_____

_____

_____

_____

_____

_____

_____

_____

_____

Daily Reflection

What habit do you need to incorporate in your life?

_____

_____

_____

_____

_____

_____

_____

_____

_____

_____

_____

_____

_____

_____

_____

_____

_____

_____

Daily Reflection

What are your strongest qualities?

_____

_____

_____

_____

_____

_____

_____

_____

_____

_____

_____

_____

_____

_____

_____

_____

_____

_____

Daily Reflection

When do you feel the most like yourself?

_____

_____

_____

_____

_____

_____

_____

_____

_____

_____

_____

_____

_____

_____

_____

_____

_____

_____

_____

Daily Reflection

What part of your life do you love most?

_____

_____

_____

_____

_____

_____

_____

_____

_____

_____

_____

_____

_____

_____

_____

_____

_____

_____

Mood Tracker

Notice your moods and how they are each day. Color each apple according to your mood of the day and notice the pattern of mood.

⬛ Happy	⬜ Sad	⬜ Angry
⬛ Confused	⬛ Loved	⬛ Scared
⬛ Anxious	⬜ Excited	⬛ Surprised

Daily Reflection

What are 10 things you are good at?

_____

_____

_____

_____

_____

_____

_____

_____

_____

_____

_____

_____

_____

_____

_____

_____

_____

_____

_____

_____

Daily Reflection

What moment do you consider to be your happiest?

_____

_____

_____

_____

_____

_____

_____

_____

_____

_____

_____

_____

_____

_____

_____

_____

_____

_____

_____

_____

Daily Reflection

What are you most grateful to have in your life?

_____

_____

_____

_____

_____

_____

_____

_____

_____

_____

_____

_____

_____

_____

_____

_____

_____

_____

Daily Reflection

Name 5 people you are grateful for in your life?

_____

_____

_____

_____

_____

_____

_____

_____

_____

_____

_____

_____

_____

_____

_____

_____

_____

_____

Daily Reflection

In what ways do you practice self-care?

_____

_____

_____

_____

_____

_____

_____

_____

_____

_____

_____

_____

_____

_____

_____

_____

_____

_____

_____

Stress Scale

Check yourself and how you are doing. On a scale of 1-10 how stressed are you and why?

10

9

8

7

6

5

4

3

2

1

    1   2   3   4   5   6   7   8   9   10

Why do you feel that level of stress

_____

_____

_____

_____

Daily Reflection

What is your favorite part of your body and why?

_____

_____

_____

_____

_____

_____

_____

_____

_____

_____

_____

_____

_____

_____

_____

_____

Daily Reflection

What are 5 things that made you smile today?

Daily Reflection

How would your best friend describe you?

_____

_____

_____

_____

_____

_____

_____

_____

_____

_____

_____

_____

_____

_____

_____

_____

_____

_____

_____

_____

_____

Daily Reflection

When do you feel the most confident?

_____

_____

_____

_____

_____

_____

_____

_____

_____

_____

_____

_____

_____

_____

_____

_____

_____

_____

_____

Daily Reflection

Write yourself a love letter.

_____

_____

_____

_____

_____

_____

_____

_____

_____

_____

_____

_____

_____

_____

_____

_____

_____

_____

Remember your 30-day Challenge?

How did it go?

_____

_____

_____

_____

_____

_____

_____

_____

_____

_____

_____

_____

_____

_____

_____

_____

_____

Thought Log

Write and record all that goes through your head. The thoughts you have and the reasons for those thoughts.

DATE

EVENTS

THOUGHTS

CONSEQUENCE

Daily Reflection

What kind words can you say to yourself today?

Daily Reflection

In what ways can you practice self-love on a daily basis?

_____

_____

_____

_____

_____

_____

_____

_____

_____

_____

_____

_____

_____

_____

_____

_____

_____

_____

_____

_____

Daily Reflection

When I think of self-love, I feel .....

_____
_____
_____
_____
_____
_____
_____
_____
_____
_____
_____
_____
_____
_____
_____
_____
_____
_____

Daily Reflection

When I think of self-love, I see ....

_____

_____

_____

_____

_____

_____

_____

_____

_____

_____

_____

_____

_____

_____

_____

_____

_____

_____

Daily Reflection

How do you show up despite not feeling like yourself?

_____

_____

_____

_____

_____

_____

_____

_____

_____

_____

_____

_____

_____

_____

_____

_____

_____

_____

_____

_____

Habits that encourage self-love

There are numerous habits that you can adopt in your day-to-day life. Some are bad for you while some are good for you. When practicing self-love, there are some habits that you should adopt to escalate your self-love process. These habits will become a part of you and stick with you for the rest of your life.

Use the habit tracker on the next page to keep track of your habits, both good and bad, and know those you need to prioritize and the habits you need to cut out.

Practice Mindfulness

Celebrate yourself

Prioritize self-care

Don't concern yourself with what others think of you

Embrace your past selves

Allow yourself to make mistakes

Habits that encourage self-love

There are numerous habits that you can adopt in your day-to-day life. Some are bad for you while some are good for you. When practicing self-love, there are some habits that you should adopt to escalate your self-love process. These habits will become a part of you and stick with you for the rest of your life.

Use the habit tracker on the next page to keep track of your habits, both good and bad, and know those you need to prioritize and the habits you need to cut out.

Your value doesn't lie in how you look

Process your fears

Learn to say NO

Let go of Toxic people

Learn to be confident

Trust yourself to follow your intuition

Habit tracker

Month:

A good way to keep track of your habits is with a habit tracker. Use this habit tracker to understand your habits and cues, and use it to build new and improved habits for long-term growth and development.

Daily Reflection

What are some negative patterns you see in yourself?

_____

_____

_____

_____

_____

_____

_____

_____

_____

_____

_____

_____

_____

_____

_____

_____

_____

_____

_____

_____

_____

Daily Reflection

Write a positive letter of advice to your future self.

_____

_____

_____

_____

_____

_____

_____

_____

_____

_____

_____

_____

_____

_____

_____

_____

_____

_____

Daily Reflection

What traits do you admire in someone?

_____

_____

_____

_____

_____

_____

_____

_____

_____

_____

_____

_____

_____

_____

_____

_____

_____

_____

_____

_____

Daily Reflection

Write out a perfect morning routine that you should stick to.

_____

_____

_____

_____

_____

_____

_____

_____

_____

_____

_____

_____

_____

_____

_____

_____

_____

_____

Daily Reflection

Did you offend yourself in any way? How did you forgive yourself?

_____

_____

_____

_____

_____

_____

_____

_____

_____

_____

_____

_____

_____

_____

_____

_____

_____

_____

_____

_____

_____

Celebrate Yourself

Celebrate yourself in any way you can think of. It's about you right now, so what will you do to keep your smile alive and increase the amount of self-love you have for yourself

Daily Reflection

What bad habits and mindsets do you need to quit?

_____

_____

_____

_____

_____

_____

_____

_____

_____

_____

_____

_____

_____

_____

_____

_____

_____

_____

_____

Daily Reflection

What is your favorite movie, comedy, or show? Why?

_____

_____

_____

_____

_____

_____

_____

_____

_____

_____

_____

_____

_____

_____

_____

_____

_____

_____

Daily Reflection

Why do you think self-worth is important?

_____

_____

_____

_____

_____

_____

_____

_____

_____

_____

_____

_____

_____

_____

_____

_____

_____

_____

_____

_____

_____

Daily Reflection

What are 5 good habits you want to start next month

Daily Reflection

What is your favorite holiday? Describe your feelings
about that holiday?

_____

_____

_____

_____

_____

_____

_____

_____

_____

_____

_____

_____

_____

_____

_____

_____

_____

_____

_____

the sun will shine again

I own my life and
I am free to make
my own choices

Daily Reflection

Take your journal to a cool and quiet place outside, with nature. Write about your feelings at the moment.

_____

_____

_____

_____

_____

_____

_____

_____

_____

_____

_____

_____

_____

_____

_____

_____

_____

_____

_____

Daily Reflection

If you could pass along positivity to the world, how would you do it?

_____

_____

_____

_____

_____

_____

_____

_____

_____

_____

_____

_____

_____

_____

_____

_____

_____

_____

_____

_____

_____

Daily Reflection

If you were to decide that you are deserving of love, how would you show up?

_____

_____

_____

_____

_____

_____

_____

_____

_____

_____

_____

_____

_____

_____

_____

_____

_____

_____

_____

Daily Reflection

What can you start doing today to show up as the person
you want to be?

_____

_____

_____

_____

_____

_____

_____

_____

_____

_____

_____

_____

_____

_____

_____

_____

_____

_____

_____

Daily Reflection

When you picture yourself happy, what do you see?

_____

_____

_____

_____

_____

_____

_____

_____

_____

_____

_____

_____

_____

_____

_____

_____

_____

_____

_____

Daily Reflection

How would you teach someone about self-love?

_____

_____

_____

_____

_____

_____

_____

_____

_____

_____

_____

_____

_____

_____

_____

_____

_____

_____

_____

_____

_____

_____

Daily Reflection

Do you think body love is important to you?

_____

_____

_____

_____

_____

_____

_____

_____

_____

_____

_____

_____

_____

_____

_____

_____

_____

_____

Daily Reflection

Where do you see yourself in the next 10 years?

_____

_____

_____

_____

_____

_____

_____

_____

_____

_____

_____

_____

_____

_____

_____

_____

_____

_____

Daily Reflection

Describe the life you want to create for yourself.

_____

_____

_____

_____

_____

_____

_____

_____

_____

_____

_____

_____

_____

_____

_____

_____

_____

_____

_____

Daily Reflection

What does a perfect day look like for you?

_____

_____

_____

_____

_____

_____

_____

_____

_____

_____

_____

_____

_____

_____

_____

_____

_____

_____

Bucket List

On your journey to self-love, you may have come across different activities that you want to try out. Use this bucket list to write out the activities and the things you want to try out. Tick each activity as you complete them.

- [ ]
- [ ]
- [ ]
- [ ]
- [ ]
- [ ]
- [ ]
- [ ]
- [ ]
- [ ]
- [ ]
- [ ]
- [ ]
- [ ]
- [ ]

Daily Reflection

What makes you feel loved and cared for?

_____

_____

_____

_____

_____

_____

_____

_____

_____

_____

_____

_____

_____

_____

_____

_____

_____

_____

Daily Reflection

What are some good things that happened to you this week?

_____

_____

_____

_____

_____

_____

_____

_____

_____

_____

_____

_____

_____

_____

_____

_____

_____

_____

Daily Reflection

How do you want people to remember you?

_____

_____

_____

_____

_____

_____

_____

_____

_____

_____

_____

_____

_____

_____

_____

_____

_____

_____

Daily Reflection

What are 5 things you couldn't live without and why?

_____

_____

_____

_____

_____

_____

_____

_____

_____

_____

_____

_____

_____

_____

_____

_____

_____

_____

_____

_____

Daily Reflection

Where do you feel closest to yourself?

Mood Tracker

Notice your moods and how they are each day. Color each balloon according to your mood of the day, for the past week, and notice the pattern of mood.

- Happy
- Sad
- Angry
- Confused
- Loved
- Scared
- Anxious
- Excited
- Surprised

Free Doodling

Use these dot grid lines to doodle whatever you want. No need to be formal. Just let your creativity flow

Free Doodling

Use these dot grid lines to doodle whatever you want. No need to be formal. Just let your creativity flow

Stress Scale

Check yourself and how you are doing. On a scale of 1-10 how stressed are you and why?

10

9

8

7

6

5

4

3

2

1

     1   2   3   4   5   6   7   8   9   10

Why do you feel that level of stress

_____

_____

_____

_____

_____

Going for the Gold

You have been on a self-love and reflection journey, and now, it is time for you to realize and recognize who you are and what you have become.

Self Assessment

Date:

My accomplishments

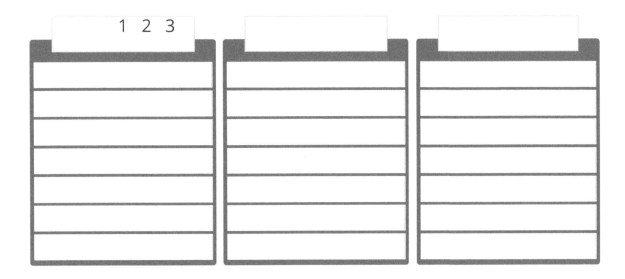

1 2 3

I felt proud when....

A positive thing I witnessed

Something that made me happy today

Self Assessment

I eat healthy foods regularly

Disagree Neutral Agree

I get an adequate amount of sleep

Disagree Neutral Agree

I exercise regularly

Disagree Neutral Agree

I rest when I'm sick

Disagree Neutral Agree

I take enough time off

Disagree Neutral Agree

I have hobbies and passions that I enjoy

Disagree Neutral Agree

I speak openly about my problems

Disagree Neutral Agree

I spend time with friends and family

Disagree Neutral Agree

I work on my personal growth

Disagree Neutral Agree

I feel grateful about many aspects of my life

Disagree Neutral Agree

I'm happy with my choices

Disagree Neutral Agree

I work on my professional skills

Disagree Neutral Agree

Made in United States
Orlando, FL
21 November 2024

54245188R10057